Healthy Eating

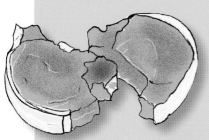

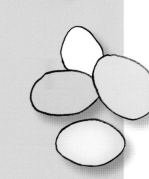

Meat
Fish and
Eggs

Susan Martineau
and Hel James

A⁺

Smart Apple Media

Published by Smart Apple Media
2140 Howard Drive West, North Mankato, MN 56003

Designed and illustrated by Helen James
Edited by Jinny Johnson

Photographs: 9 Mark Peterson/Corbis; 10-11 Ed Lallo/Zuma/Corbis; 13 Bohemian Nomad
Picturemakers/Corbis; 15 Robert Dowling/Corbis; 16 Owen Franken/Corbis; 17 DiMaggio/Kalish/Corbis;
18 Tim Thompson/Corbis; 21 Macduff Everton/Corbis; 22-23 Jeffrey L Rotman/Corbis;
24-25 Paul A Souders/Corbis; 27 PhotoCuisine/Corbis; 29 David Reed/Corbis:
Front cover: Envision/Corbis

Printed in Thailand

Library of Congress Cataloging-in-Publication Data

Martineau, Susan.
Healthy eating. Meat, fish, and eggs / by Susan Martineau
p. cm.
Includes index.
ISBN-13: 978-1-58340-893-3
1. Meat—Juvenile literature. 2. Fish as food—Juvenile literature. 3. Eggs as food—Juvenile literature. I.
Title. II. Title: Meat, fish, and eggs.

TX373.M3155 2006
641.3'06—dc22   2006008868

First Edition

9 8 7 6 5 4 3 2 1

Contents

Food for health

Our bodies are like amazing machines.
Just like machines, we need the right
kind of fuel to give us energy and
to keep us working properly.

If we don't eat the kind of food
we need to keep us healthy we
may become ill or feel tired and
grumpy. Our bodies do not like it
if we eat too much of one kind of
food, such as cakes or chips.

We need a balanced diet.
That means eating different
kinds of good food in the
right amounts.

You'll be surprised at how much
there is to know about where our
food comes from and why some
kinds of food are better for us
than others. Finding out about
food is great fun and very tasty!

I'm hungry.
I wonder what's
for dinner.

Chicken, fish, and eggs all contain lots of **protein**.

Let's go and find out.

Protein-rich foods help keep us healthy.

A balanced meal!

The good things, or **nutrients**, that our bodies need come from different kinds of food. Let's look at what your plate should have on it. It all looks delicious!

Rice, bread, and pasta

These foods contain **carbohydrates** and they give us energy. They are also called starchy foods. About a third of our food should come from this group.

Fruits and vegetables

Rice, bread, and pasta

Chicken with rice and vegetables is a great balanced meal.

6

Fruits and vegetables

These are full of great **vitamins**, **minerals**, and **fiber**. They do all kinds of useful jobs in your body to help keep you healthy. About a third of our food should come from this group.

Meat, fish, and eggs

Protein from these helps your body grow and repair itself. They are body-building foods and you need to eat some of them every day.

Milk, yogurt, and cheese

These dairy foods give us protein and **calcium** to make strong bones and teeth.

Sugar and fats

Eat only small amounts of these. Too much can be bad for our teeth and make us overweight.

Milk, yogurt, and cheese

Sugar and fats

Meat, fish, and eggs

Water

We need to drink at least six glasses of water every day.

Body-building foods

We need body-building foods that have protein so we can grow muscles, bone, hair, and skin. Protein repairs our bodies if we are ill or injured.

Who eats fish? Who eats meat?

I have lentil and vegetable stew.

Meat, fish, and eggs are fantastic protein foods. If you don't want to eat meat, you can get protein from **dairy foods**, nuts, pulses (like lentils and beans), and tofu, which is made from soy beans. People who don't eat meat are called vegetarians.

Butchers and restaurants buy meat from a meat market like this one.

Who is a vegetarian?

I have a lamb chop and vegetables.

I have cod with tomato sauce.

You don't have to eat steak three times a day to get all the protein you need. If you are eating a balanced meal, your body will be getting plenty of body-building goodness.

9

A beefy treat

Beef is the meat we get from cows. Cows kept for their meat are called beef cattle. There are cattle farms all over the world. When the animals are big enough to be used for meat, they are taken in special trucks to a market to be sold.

Steaks, such as sirloin and rump, come from the back of the animal.

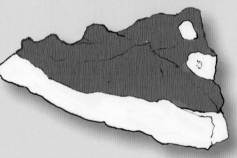

Meat from the legs and front is good for stews.

Beef is full of protein, **iron**, **zinc**, and B vitamins. Iron keeps our blood healthy and zinc helps us fight off illness. B vitamins help our bodies turn our food into energy.

Fat check

Beef is a fatty meat so we should not eat too much of it. Look for pieces of meat that are labeled **lean**. This means they have less fat in them.

You don't need to eat a lot of beef. Small amounts of meat with some vegetables in a stir-fry make a great balanced meal.

Hearty stews have pieces of meat and lots of healthy vegetables, too.

11

Sheep and lamb

Lamb is the meat that comes from sheep.
Sheep are also kept for their wool and milk.
A mother sheep can have up to three lambs a year.
When the lambs are old enough, the farmer takes
them to stores to be sold as meat.

Sheep live in large groups called **flocks**. In some countries, such as Australia and New Zealand, there are thousands of sheep living on giant farms called **sheep stations**.

Lamb gives us the same goodness, or nutrients, as beef and is very tasty. But we should not eat it too often as it also has a lot of fat in it.

Add vegetables such as onions, peppers and tomatoes to pieces of lamb to make kebabs — a delicious balanced meal.

You can buy leg of lamb as well as shoulder of lamb and lamb chops.

Roast lamb is delicious, but it's best to trim off the fat!

Pigs and pork

Pork is the meat we get from pigs. Some pig farmers keep their pigs outside. The pigs only go indoors to sleep or have their babies. Other farmers keep their pigs in big buildings and they don't go outside at all. Some people think that the pork from the outside, or **free-range**, pigs tastes better.

Bacon

Pork fillet

Pork is full of protein and other nutrients but some pork, such as a pork chop, is very fatty. Pork is also made into sausages, ham, and bacon and these also contain a lot of fat. Pork fillet, or tenderloin, is quite lean and is the healthiest way to eat pork.

Slices of ham

Pork chops

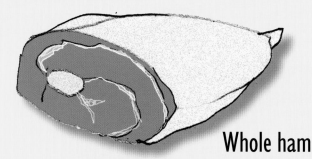

Whole ham

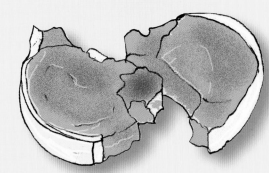

A mother pig can give birth to two litters of piglets
a year, with as many as 12 in each litter. The piglets
drink their mother's milk and they grow very fast. They
are sold for meat when they are about six months old.

Meat for keeps

Before refrigerators were invented, it was difficult to keep meat fresh. People had to think of ways to prevent it from going bad. They used to **cure**, or keep, meat by putting it into salty water, or they rubbed it with salt and then dried it. Sometimes the meat was smoked over a fire.

This piece of pork is being rubbed with salt to preserve it.

Some meat is still salted and smoked in this way today. The trouble is that these meats are not very good for us. They have lots of salt, fat, and other chemicals in them. They are best eaten only once in a while.

Can you count how many hams are hanging from the ceiling in this shop?

Ham

There are many different kinds of ham. See how many you can find when you go to the store.

Bacon

Bacon is sold in slices called **rashers**. The bacon is salted and sometimes smoked, too.

Salami

Salami is made from pork or beef.

Meat with a difference

Other animals are also kept for their meat. It might seem quite strange to eat creatures such as ostriches, deer, and buffalo, but their meat is very good for us. This meat has lots of protein, vitamins, and minerals but less fat than beef, lamb, and pork.

The biggest bird in the world

The ostrich is certainly bigger than a chicken, but its meat is just as tasty.

Liver

Herds of deer

The meat we get from deer is called **venison**.

Lambs' kidneys

Buffalo beef

These animals are kept not only for their meat but for their milk, too.

We can also get meat from the inside parts of animals. This is called **offal**. The liver, heart, and kidneys of animals are very good for us because they contain lots of vitamins.

Pieces of kidney are used in steak and kidney pie.

19

All about chicken

Chickens are farmed all over the world for their eggs and their meat. Chicken farms that keep the birds for their meat are called **broiler farms**. Chickens and other birds which are farmed for us to eat, such as turkeys, geese, and ducks, are often called poultry.

Which one of these delicious dishes would you choose?

Chicken meat is very good for us. It gives our bodies protein but has less fat in it than beef, lamb, and pork. It does not contain quite as much iron or zinc, but it has lots of B vitamins to keep us healthy.

Chicken soup

Tandoori chicken

On some broiler farms, the chickens live inside huge buildings and are given special food to make them grow quickly. On free-range broiler farms, the chickens can go outside during the day and scratch for their own food. They come indoors at night to get away from the foxes!

Roast chicken

Chicken salad baguette

Food from the sea

Fish is a great way to eat protein. It also gives our bodies vitamins and minerals. There are so many types of delicious fish to choose. Try to eat fish about twice a week if you can.

White fish

Cod, haddock, plaice, sole, turbot, and halibut are all white fish. Their flesh (or meat) has hardly any fat in it. White fish can be cooked in different ways. Grilled, baked, or steamed fish is best for us. Deep-frying fish in oil is not healthy.

Freshly frozen

Fish should be eaten soon after it has been caught. Freezing it is a way of keeping it fresh longer. A lot of fish is frozen on **factory ships** as soon as it is caught.

Fillets of fish are good to eat.

They are tasty and there are no bones!

Bream

Cod

Plaice

Haddock

Red mullet

23

Oily fish

Salmon, trout, herrings, and sardines are all oily fish. Oily fish is very good for you because it contains lots of the vitamins A and D as well as protein. The oil in the fish also helps to keep you healthy.

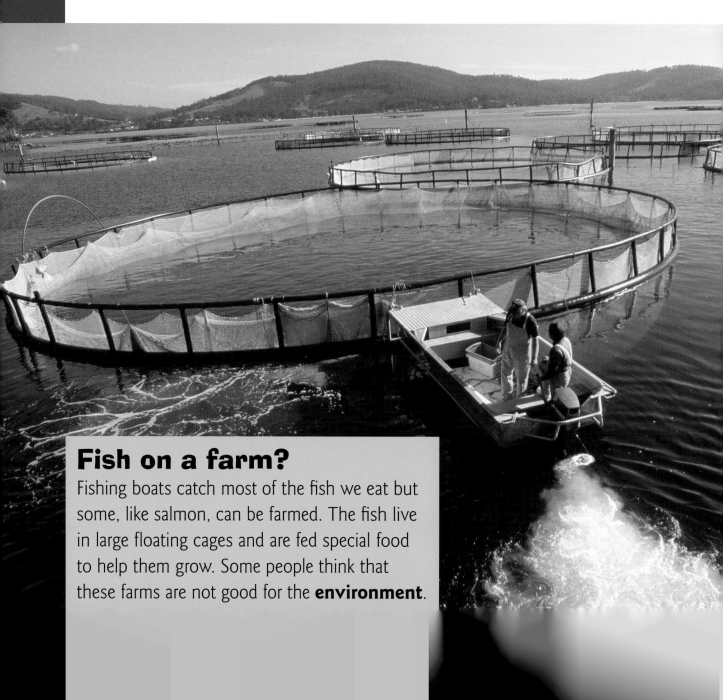

Fish on a farm?

Fishing boats catch most of the fish we eat but some, like salmon, can be farmed. The fish live in large floating cages and are fed special food to help them grow. Some people think that these farms are not good for the **environment**.

Sardine

Mackerel

Anchovy

Sea trout

Salmon

Fish in a can

Oily fish, such as salmon and sardines, can be put into cans and stored for a long time. Look in your cupboard and see what kinds of canned fish you have.

Fish in a shell

Shellfish are not really fish, but different kinds of sea creatures. All have a tough shell to protect their body. There are many kinds of shellfish such as mussels, crabs, and prawns. See how many kinds you and your friends can name. How many have you tried eating?

Prawns

Shellfish is full of protein and vitamins, but it must be eaten when it is very fresh. It is often frozen before being sent to the stores so it will last longer.

Clams

Clams taste great in a soup called a chowder.

Mussels and prawns are used to make a delicious Spanish dish called paella.

You can eat oysters fresh from the shell.

Oysters

Prawns

Mussels

Lobster

Crab

Crabs and lobsters are cooked and then served in their shells.

Excellent eggs

A chicken lays an egg nearly every day. Egg farmers keep chickens to lay eggs for us to eat. The eggs we eat are not **fertilized** and do not have chicks inside them.

Look what's in an egg!

Iron for your blood

Vitamin A for your eyes

Zinc to fight off illness

Body-building protein

B vitamins to keep your body working properly

Vitamin D and calcium for making strong bones and teeth

Power pack

All eggs are checked and sorted into sizes before being packed into boxes for the stores. An egg is full of nutrients for our bodies.

Thousands of battery chickens are kept together in rows of very small cages. Many people prefer to buy eggs that come from free-range hens.

Some egg farms are free-range. The chickens can wander about outside and find food. They lay their eggs inside a hen house where they sleep at night. Other farms keep thousands of chickens inside giant buildings in rows of small cages. These are called battery farms. The eggs from these chickens roll onto a **conveyor belt**.

Egg quiz
Ask your friends how they like to eat eggs. What is the most popular dish? Do they prefer eggs poached, scrambled, or made into omelettes?

Words to remember

broiler farms   Chicken farms where the birds are kept for their meat.

calcium   A mineral that helps build healthy bones and teeth.

carbohydrates   Starches and sugars in food that give us energy. Carbohydrate foods are rice, pasta, bread, and potatoes.

conveyor belt   The moving part of a machine that carries things from one part of a farm or factory to another.

cure   To salt, smoke, or dry meat or fish so that it will keep for longer.

dairy foods   Foods made from milk, such as cheese, butter, cream, and yogurt.

environment   The world around us.

factory ships   Fishing boats that catch large amounts of fish, clean them, and freeze them.

fertilized   When an egg is fertilized, a chick will grow inside it.

fiber   This is found in plant foods like grains and vegetables. It helps our insides work properly.

flock   A large group of animals.

free-range   Free-range animals are allowed to live and roam outdoors.

iron   A mineral in food that we need to keep our blood healthy.

lean　Meat without fat on it.

minerals　Nutrients in food that help our bodies work properly. Calcium, iron, and zinc are minerals.

nutrients　Parts of food that your body needs to make energy, to grow healthily, and to repair itself.

offal　Meat from the insides of animals, such as the kidneys, liver, and heart.

protein　Body-building food that makes our bodies grow well and stay healthy.

rashers　Slices of bacon are called rashers.

sheep stations　Huge sheep farms in New Zealand and Australia.

venison　The meat from deer.

vitamins　Nutrients in food that help our bodies work properly. Vitamin A is good for our eyes. There are several B vitamins. They help turn our food into energy and keep our muscles, skin, and blood healthy. Vitamin D helps our bodies use calcium to make strong bones and teeth.

zinc　This mineral helps our body fight off illness and repair itself when we are injured.

Index

Web sites

Learn which foods make a healthy heart.
http://www.healthyfridge.org/

Test your nutritional knowledge with quizzes, dietary guidelines, and a glossary of terms.
http://www.exhibits.pacsci.org/nutrition/

Find out how to have a healthy diet without eating meat.
http://www.vrg.org/family/kidsindex.htm

Get the facts about fast food restaurants and tips for making healthy choices.
http://library.thinkquest.org/4485/

Take the 5-a-day challenge and learn about fruits and vegetables with puzzles, music, and games.
http://www.dole5aday.com/

Discover ten tips for a healthy lifestyle.
http://www.fitness.gov/l0tips.htm